Bure Valley Railway

Gerry Balding

First published in 2017
Second Edition in 2021

British Library Cataloguing in Publication Data

A catalogue record for this book is available from the British Library.

ISBN 978 1 85794 580 5

Silver Link Books
Mortons Media Group Limited
Media Centre
Morton Way
Horncastle
LN9 6JR
Tel/Fax: 01507 529535
email: sohara@mortons.co.uk
Website: www.nostalgiacollection.com

Printed and bound in the Czech Republic

All photographs © Gerry Balding unless otherwise stated.

Contents

Frontispiece: John of Gaunt and *Wroxham Broad* at Wroxham, April 2016.

Introduction
by Andrew Barnes

The 15-inch-gauge Bure Valley Railway is built on the trackbed of the former East Norfolk Railway branch from Wroxham to Aylsham, which opened in 1880. It was later extended to join the Wymondham to Wells-Next-The-Sea branch at County School. The East Norfolk Railway was absorbed in 1882 by the Great Eastern Railway, which in turn became part of the London & North Eastern Railway in 1923. Traffic was never heavy, although during the Second World War there was a resurgence as the line served several local airbases, including RAF Coltishall.

After 1948 the line was operated by British Railways. Passenger traffic ceased in 1952, but some freight services lingered, including grain for the Scottish whisky industry and concrete beams from a factory at Lenwade accessed at Themelthorpe via a new chord built to the former Midland & Great Northern line to Norwich City. The concrete beam traffic ceased in late 1981 and British Rail formally closed the line on 6 January 1982. The last standard gauge trains over the line were track-lifting specials during early 1984.

Many thought this was the end of the line for the route as a railway. However, in 1986 the idea of reviving the line, as well as providing a public footpath, was promoted by Broadland District Council as a joint venture between the

private and public sectors. A gauge of 15 inches was chosen, as it would only require half of the trackbed and would therefore leave space for the footpath. The contract to build the railway was won by John Edwards and Robert Hudson, who were automotive engineers in Great Yarmouth. To raise the required capital they went into partnership with RKF Limited, which at the time owned a theme park near Lowestoft. Construction of the line was started on 8 May 1989, with Fred Dibnah as guest, and progressed quickly, being officially opened on 10 July 1990.

While the railway had built 20 modern and comfortable carriages and well-equipped station facilities, it did not have the required capital or time to obtain steam locomotives. As a result locomotives were hired in from the Romney, Hythe & Dymchurch Railway for the first year. The engines returned to Kent in early 1991 and the BVR started to acquire its own motive power from a variety of sources. The new arrivals struggled to maintain services until motive power designed specifically to meet the demands of the BVR arrived in the form of the 'ZBs' in spring 1994. Since then the railway has built additional steam locomotives and constantly improved them, and today they form a reliable and powerful fleet well suited to the line.

During the first ten years of existence the railway experienced severe financial difficulties and had five different sets of owners. In 1991 the original company went into receivership and the line was very near to closure. What was needed was stability and sound management, and this came in 2001 when the line was acquired by a small group of railway enthusiasts from a business background.

The railway has now enjoyed success and stability under the same ownership for 19 years. The company is run by a small Board of Directors and staff supported by a very active team of volunteers and the Friends of the Bure Valley Railway (a very active supporters association). No dividends are paid to shareholders and all profits are reinvested in developing and securing the long-term future of the railway and improving facilities. This has enabled the railway to improve the experience for passengers.

The Bure Valley Railway runs between the very attractive market town of Aylsham and Wroxham, 'The Capital of the Broads', passing through the villages of Brampton, Buxton and Coltishall. Aylsham is the headquarters of the railway, with the engine shed, workshops, museum and shop; the Whistlestop Café is also located here as well as the signal box, which controls the radio signalling for the entire line.

At Wroxham the terminus is conveniently situated alongside the Abellio Greater Anglia Railways' 'Bittern Line' from Norwich to Sheringham. The town is the popular centre of the Norfolk Broads holiday industry, with attractive river tours and some superb shops and restaurants.

Andrew Barnes

Useful information

To contact the Bure Valley Railway

By post, please write to:
Bure Valley Railway,
Aylsham Station,
Norwich Road,
Aylsham
Norfolk
NR11 6BW

By phone: 01263 733 858
By Fax: 01263 733 814

For timetable, Friends' membership details, newsletter information and more please visit the railway's web site:

www.bvrw.co.uk

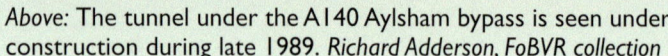

Above: The tunnel under the A140 Aylsham bypass is seen under construction during late 1989. *Richard Adderson, FoBVR collection*

Above right: The station building at Coltishall is seen in early 1990; this was the headquarters for building the line. The works train can be seen on the right, and the hopper wagon is still part of the BVR permanent way (PW) fleet. *Richard Adderson, FoBVR collection*

Right: In early 1990 Aylsham station is under construction. The steelwork for the train shed is in place with the roof of the workshop/running shed visible behind. The area on the left is now the Whistlestop Café. *Richard Adderson, FoBVR collection*

Samson and *Winston Churchill*, on hire from the Romney, Hythe & Dymchurch Railway, haul the first passenger train into Aylsham on opening day, 10 July 1990. *BVR News collection*

Samson runs off the turntable at Aylsham on 26 August 1990. The original goods shed still stood at that time, and there is a marked lack of tree growth compared to the present day. The goods shed was demolished in 1991 to make way for a sheltered housing development, and the right foreground is the location of the current signal box.

Samson arrives at Aylsham with a train from Wroxham in August 1990. The BVR station was built on the site of the old goods sidings alongside the Norwich to Cromer and Sheringham 'Bittern Line'. In this scene a Metro-Cammell Class 101 DMU (heritage traction in its own right now!), forming a Sheringham to Norwich working, slows for Wroxham station.

Above: A Bure Valley Railway headboard is displayed on *Wroxham Broad* (BVR No 1).

Right: The railway runs popular combined train/river cruise trips on the Norfolk Broads in conjunction with a local pleasure cruise company. Passengers can buy a combined ticket and travel by train from Aylsham to Wroxham followed by a cruise on the Norfolk Broads. In April 2015 *John of Gaunt* (BVR No 8) departs from Aylsham with the 'Bure Valley Boat Train'.

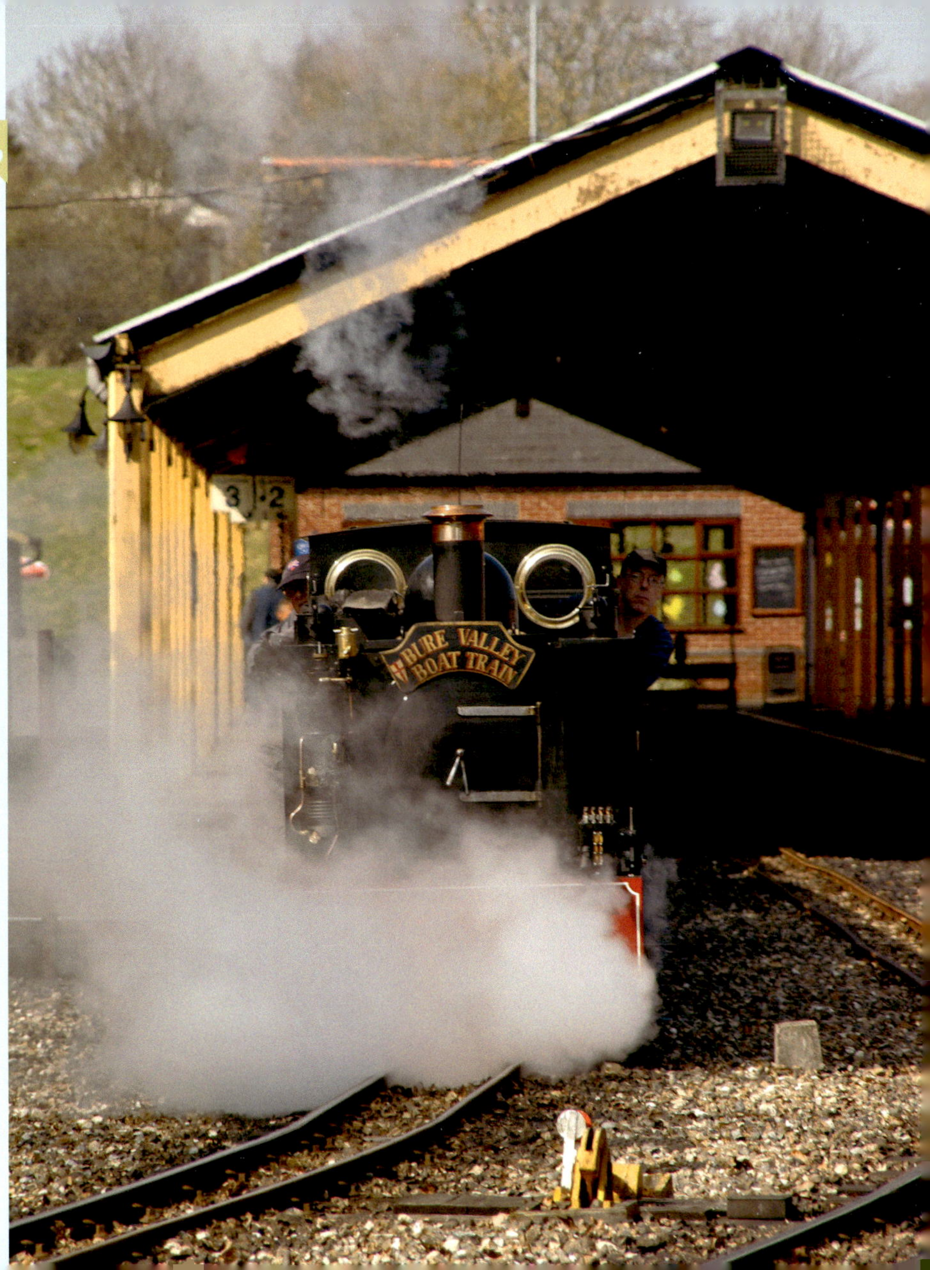

Every December the 'Steam Trains to Santa' are extremely popular with families and are often sold out weeks in advance. After a steam-hauled trip from Wroxham, guests meet Father Christmas in his grotto at Aylsham. In December 2018, Father Christmas greets *Spitfire* (BVR No 7) and *Wroxham Broad* (BVR No 1) as they arrive at Aylsham.

Left: Every October the railway marks Halloween with a week-long series of 'Spooky Express' services. Here *Mark Timothy* heads towards Wroxham.

Right: During January 2016 *Spitfire* (BVR No 7) is seen working a charter using 'The Broadsman' headboard. The name reflects the title of a crack LNER express that used to run from London's Liverpool Street to the Norfolk Broads. The train is leaving Coltishall bound for Wroxham.

February half-term sees the railway's popular 'Teddy Express' week. In February 2016 *Mark Timothy* departs from Coltishall with a train for Wroxham.

25th Anniversary

During the summer of 2015 the Bure Valley Railway celebrated its Silver Jubilee. The celebrations were held in two parts. From 10 to 12 July there was a 25th Anniversary Gala, on the first day of which a 'Steam Back In Time' day was held where passengers paid the same fares as on the opening day back in 1990. It had been hoped that the two original hire locos from the RH&DR would attend, but *Samson* was undergoing a major overhaul. Instead *Green Goddess* proved to be a popular substitute when it visited the Bure Valley together with *Winston Churchill*.

On 10 July *Winston Churchill* (left) and *Green Goddess* are prepared at Aylsham before double-heading the anniversary special.

Above: The anniversary special passes Aylsham signal box.

Above right: Winston Churchill is turned on the turntable at Wroxham.

Right: Green Goddess nears Buxton .

Below: On the same day *Green Goddess* pilots *Winston Churchill* into Buxton on 11 July. The significance of the 'Brothers' headboard is that for the first time two brothers drove a double-headed train hauled by RH&DR locos. Visiting driver Ian Botting from the RH&DR was at the controls of *Green Goddess* with his brother Alan, also from the RH&DR, driving *Winston Churchill.*

Left: Present at the Gala weekend were the two former RH&DR drivers who had driven the first steam-hauled train on 10 July 1990: the late Richard Batten (left) and Derek Walsh. Richard, who drove *Winston Churchill,* came up from Kent, while Derek, who drove *Samson,* flew in especially for the anniversary weekend from the Shetlands.

The second part of the 25th Anniversary celebrations was held over the weekend of 26 and 27 September, with the 'Steam in Miniature' event. The visiting locos on this occasion were *Northern Rock* from the Ravenglass & Eskdale Railway, and SR&RL No 24 from the Cleethorpes Coast Light Railway.

Left: SR&RL No 24 is seen here in the yard at Aylsham. Technical difficulties prevented it from being steamed, but it made a welcome return to one of its old homes, having been part of the BVR fleet from 1991 until 1997 when it finally departed for Cleethorpes.

On 27 September *Northern Rock* is seen approaching Buxton.

Locomotives

When the railway opened in 1990, it only owned one locomotive, which was the diesel locomotive (BVR 3) built to construct the line. It therefore turned to the Romney, Hythe & Dymchurch Railway to borrow locomotives and drivers to operate services in the early years. The Romney locomotives returned home early in 1991, and since then the Bure Valley has built up a powerful fleet of steam locomotives that have been specifically designed and built to work on the demanding 9-mile route between Aylsham and Wroxham.

Above: **BVR No 1** *Wroxham Broad*

This is a 2-6-4 tank locomotive, painted in Caledonian light blue livery. It was originally built in 1964 by Guest Engineering as a steam-outline internal-combustion 2-6-2 tank locomotive, and was named *Tracy-Jo*. Following a nomadic life, it came to the Bure Valley early in 1991 and was rebuilt as a steam locomotive the following year by Winson Engineering; upon completion it was renamed *Wroxham Broad*. The locomotive is now owned by the Bure Valley Railway No 1 Preservation Group and is on long-term loan to the railway.

Left: **BVR No 6** *Blickling Hall*

The design of this 'ZB' Class 2-6-2 tender locomotive is inspired by the Indian Railway 'ZB' Class of locomotives. Although a half-size replica, it boasts two-thirds of the tractive effort of the original. It was designed and built specifically for the railway by Winson Engineering and was delivered to the railway at Easter 1994. Since then *Blickling Hall* has undergone two major overhauls and a number of improvements to both performance and efficiency. BVR No 6 returned to steam in December 2016 following an extensive overhaul that lasted three years, and now wears a livery of Great Eastern blue.

BVR No 7 *Spitfire*

Another 'ZB' Class 2-6-2 tender locomotive, it is similar in design to *Blickling Hall*, and was delivered to the railway in May 1994. It has a livery of British Railways lined green, and was named in 1997 in recognition of the role played by the Spitfire aircraft that flew from many local bases during the Second World War. Like BVR No 6, *Spitfire* has undergone two major overhauls and a number of improvements to both her performance and efficiency.

BVR No 8 *John of Gaunt* (previously known as *Thunder*)

This is a 2-6-2 tank locomotive based on the chassis and mechanics of the two 'ZB' tender locomotives, and the outline is based on the Vale of Rheidol Railway tank locomotives. It was built in the BVR's workshop at Aylsham during 1996/7 from components originally manufactured and supplied by Winson Engineering. *John of Gaunt* is currently painted in LNWR blackberry black livery. It was originally oil-fired and was rather noisy, hence the name *Thunder*. The locomotive was subsequently converted to coal-firing in 2008 when the price of fuel oil rose dramatically. Since then, it has received a number of improvements to both performance and efficiency, undertaken in the workshop at Aylsham.

In 2014 the locomotive was named *John of Gaunt* after the Lord of the Manor of Aylsham during the 14th century.

BVR No 9 *Mark Timothy*

Mark Timothy is a 2-6-4 tank locomotive based on the chassis and mechanics of the other 'ZB' Class locomotives. Originally built as a County Donegal-style tank locomotive by Winson Engineering in 1999, it was unable to operate in this form and was sent to Alan Keef Limited to be modified and rebuilt. BVR No 9 returned to the railway in 2003 and entered passenger traffic in July the following year; it is the newest loco on the railway. In its rebuilt state No 9 resembles a Kitson tank locomotive of the Leek & Manifold Railway and carries a madder lake livery. It has been very successful in this form.

The locomotive was named *Mark Timothy* in memory of the owner's son, who sadly passed away at a young age.

John of Gaunt, *Spitfire* and *Wroxham Broad* pose at Wroxham in April 2016.

Spitfire and *Wroxham Broad* on shed at Aylsham.

BVR No 3 *2nd Air Division U.S.A.A.F.*
(previously known as *Buxton Mill*)

This locomotive was designed and built by John Edwards and delivered in May 1989 to assist in the construction of the line. It has a single cab and is powered by a Bedford diesel engine with hydraulic transmission. After several changes of livery over the years, it now carries a golden yellow ochre livery. BVR No 3 is used all through the year on passenger duties, permanent way trains, route-learning courses and general work.

After completing a major refit in the autumn of 1998, the locomotive was named *2nd Air Division U.S.A.A.F.* in honour of American pilots who flew from local airbases during the Second World War.

BVR No 4 *Rusty*

This locomotive was originally built by Hudson-Hunslet in 1954 as a 2-foot-gauge four-wheel industrial locomotive. It was partially rebuilt and re-gauged to the 15-inch gauge by apprentices at Eagit Ltd, but was subsequently completely rebuilt by a small and dedicated group of the Friends of the Bure Valley Railway.

Rusty is fitted with the diesel engine from a Peugeot 205 car with hydraulic drive. Its main use is as Aylsham yard pilot, but it also finds use on track work and as motive power for the railway's flail machine.

The locomotive is owned by the Friends of the Bure Valley Railway and was handed over for use on the BVR in October 2004.

BVR No 5

This Lister diesel-mechanical loco was originally built to the 2-foot gauge and used on Fisons' peat railways on the Somerset Levels. The top framework was added late in the 1970s and had canvas drop-down sheeting to protect the operator from inclement weather. It arrived on the BVR in 1993 and was subsequently converted to the 15-inch gauge. No 5 is mainly used for shunting at Aylsham. In early years on the BVR a wooden outer body was added to give the loco a tram-like appearance.

Following an overhaul undertaken by a group of dedicated volunteers, BVR No 5 was restored to working condition and its 1970s appearance, and returned to service in May 2016.

Rolling stock

When the railway opened in 1990 a fleet of purpose-built and well-appointed saloon coaches was supplied. There are currently 19 twin-bogie carriages, each of which has five bays seating four passengers each. Over the years these have been refurbished and modernised, including the fitting of new roofs. The railway has also built six new coaches, each of which is fully accessible for wheelchairs. All the coaches are fully enclosed with upholstered seating and fitted with electric lighting. Electric heating is provided during the colder months.

Above: Coach No 31 is a standard 'Special Saloon'. There are six of these coaches, all designed and built for the railway to be fully accessible for wheelchairs, allowing wheelchair-users and able-bodied passengers to enjoy the journey together.

Above: This is one of the railway's standard saloon coaches. It has recently been refurbished with new end windows and a new roof.

Above: This is the interior of 'Special Saloon' No 33. There are fold-down bench seats to allow spaces for wheelchairs or pushchairs.

Above: Coach No 20 is unique. Although it is a standard coach, it has been fitted with a guard's compartment and a parcels compartment. There are also two open compartments with seating for four passengers.

Above: When the BVR opened it built two guard's vans, known as PCs (power cars), to carry both the guard and the original electro-pneumatic braking equipment used in the early years. This braking system was eventually replaced by an air brake system using air generated by the locomotives. The redundant equipment was removed from the two vans and they became solely guard's vans. The two original vans (Nos 81 and 82) remain in traffic to this day, having been refurbished and modified over the last 30 years.

Left: The railway has built two new mobile generator vans (Coaches 40 and 41) to provide electric heating to trains in the colder months. Van 40 was designed and built in-house at Aylsham during late 2016. Van 41 (pictured) was built to a similar specification and entered service in February 2019. Both vans are fitted with a 45KVA Hyundai generator mounted on a four-wheel chassis similar to those used on the guards' vans. These vans have enabled the railway to run two electrically heated sets to improve capacity and flexibility.

Monster is the railway's permanent way support van, and was built specially for the BVR in 2001 by Ken Girvan & Son.

Right: On 7 December 2013 *Mark Timothy* waits with a 'Santa Special' for Wroxham.

Aylsham

Aylsham is the headquarters of the Bure Valley Railway. The original station buildings and goods yard were demolished in May 1989 to make way for the new station facilities and car park. The site is dominated by the large overall roof spanning the two main platforms and centre release road. Here are located the workshop, running shed and the operational centre. Facilities for passengers include a well-stocked gift and model railway shop, the Whistlestop Café and the shop of the Friends of the Bure Valley Railway.

Right: Mark Timothy awaits departure on 10 July 2015, with *Spitfire* on the turntable.

Above: John of Gaunt awaits departure on 28 September 2015.

Right: On 11 September 2016 *Spitfire* departs for Wroxham.

When it opened, the railway was equipped with a workshop/running shed, but over the years it outgrew these facilities and in early 2014 a large running shed extension was built. This allowed the original shed to become a separate self-contained workshop area. The Bure Valley is well equipped to undertake repairs and overhauls of both locomotives and rolling stock. During 2019 *John of Gaunt* underwent a comprehensive overhaul, returning to traffic in February 2020.

The signal box at Aylsham is the nerve centre of the railway's operations. All train movements are controlled from here by a radio dispatch system. *John of Gaunt* departs on 7 April 2015.

The driver of *Wroxham Broad* and the controller exchange movement orders as the train enters Aylsham station on 27 September 2015.

Aylsham

TICKET OFFICE
CAFE
SHOP
TOILETS

Brampton

Buxton

PLATFORM ONLY
GREAT WALKS

PLATFORM ONLY
GREAT WALKS

On 12 July 2016 *John of Gaunt* picks up speed as she descends towards Aylsham Tunnel.

The 250-yard cut-and-cover tunnel under the A140 Aylsham bypass is Norfolk's only rail tunnel currently in use. The original standard gauge line crossed the road on the level, but a condition of building the BVR was that this crossing was replaced by a tunnel, due to the volume of traffic on the busy road. On 12 July 2016 *Spitfire* emerges from the tunnel and starts the climb towards the terminus at Aylsham.

PLATFORM ONLY
GREAT WALKS

Coltishall

Wroxham BVR

Wroxham Network Rail

TICKET OFFICE
SNACKS
SMALL SHOP
TOILETS

THIS WAY TO
THE BOATS!

Aylsham to Brampton

Below: At the other end of the tunnel, *Mark Timothy* bursts out of the portal with a returning 'Santa Special' to Wroxham on 20 December 2016.

Right: Wroxham Broad is also seen leaving the tunnel with a train to Wroxham on 7 April 2015.

Below right: Spitfire heads towards Aylsham near the tunnel on 10 July 2015.

Left: At Spratt's Green, approximately a mile from Aylsham, the line crosses the first of two minor roads by ungated crossings. Here *Wroxham Broad* slows for the crossing in April 2019.

Below: Mark Timothy crosses the road at Spratt's Green bound for Aylsham on 20 December 2016.

A rare double-header: *Spitfire* and *Wroxham Broad* whistle through the crossing at Spratt's Green on 3 September 2016.

Spitfire approaches Spratt's Green with a demonstration permanent way train in September 2008.

BURE VALLEY RAILWAY

Brampton

The line is single track throughout with passing loops at Brampton, Hautbois (pronounced 'Hobbis') and Coltishall. Brampton is 3 miles from Aylsham and there is a single-platform halt where trains stop by request.

Right: On 20 December 2016 *Mark Timothy* pulls away from Brampton with a 'Santa Special' for Aylsham.

Below: Blickling Hall passes the halt at Brampton with a train for Wroxham in February 2018.

Below: Mark Timothy pulls away from Brampton loop on 25 August 2015 with a train for Wroxham.

Left: The loop at Brampton is located between two road underbridges. Here *Spitfire* pulls out of the loop towards Buxton on 3 August 2015.

Buxton

Buxton is the largest village on the line and is served by a single-platform request halt. When the BVR was planned, there was opposition to the railway from local residents, so no station was to be provided. This opposition diminished over time and a small halt was built before the line opened to the public. The halt is located on the site of the former standard gauge goods siding. The original station building still stands but is in private ownership.

Blickling Hall slows for Buxton with an 'Easter Eggspress' on 19 April 2019.

On 23 March 2008 *Mark Timothy* starts to climb Buxton bank on its way to Brampton.

On 30 March 2015 *2nd Air Division U.S.A.A.F.* enters Buxton with a train bound for Wroxham, replacing a failed steam loco.

On 28 September 2016 *Mark Timothy* departs from Buxton bound for Aylsham.

Above: Mark Timothy passes the snowy halt at Buxton on 19 December 2009 with an Aylsham-bound 'Santa Special'.

On 1 May 2010 *Blickling Hall* departs from Buxton for Coltishall.

On 30 March 2016 *Spitfire* slows for Buxton. The original station building and platform can be seen on the right.

Buxton to Coltishall

The second large structure on the line is the bridge over the River Bure near Buxton, where the railway and footpath share the decking. Here *Spitfire* heads towards Coltishall in 2019. *BVR collection*

The second crossing loop is at Hautbois, situated alongside tranquil meadows leading down to the River Bure. This represents the halfway point of the journey and is frequently used as a crossing point for trains. *Spitfire* heads towards Hautbois Loop (just visible in the distance) in 2019. *BVR collection*.

On 30 March 2016 *Mark Timothy* passes a train for Wroxham as it leaves Hautbois loop bound for Aylsham.

The tranquil location of Hautbois loop is shown here on the same day as *Spitfire* departs towards Coltishall…

… and again on 24 June 2015 as *John of Gaunt* arrives from Coltishall.

Left: On 21 August 2018, *Mark Timothy* approaches Hautbois Hall Crossing with a train for Aylsham.

Below left: On 22 August 2017, *Blickling Hall* passes under the road bridge at Adam & Eve and starts the climb to Runway Curve.

Below: On 12 August 2008 *2nd Air Division U.S.A.A.F.*, heading a Wroxham train, descends through the cutting at Seven Acres on the approach to Coltishall. The footpath that runs alongside the railway for its entire length can be seen on the left of the train.

Coltishall

The third passing loop on the line is at Coltishall, where the central island platform allows passengers to change trains. The station building from standard gauge days still stands in private ownership, while the goods yard has recently had new housing built on it. The Wroxham end of the station is dominated by a bridge carrying the main Norwich to North Walsham road over the railway.

Above: On 7 June 2016 *Wroxham Broad* waits at Coltishall with a train for Aylsham.

Left: 2nd Air Division U.S.A.A.F. waits to depart for Wroxham on 30 May 2016. The station building can be seen on the right.

Right: On 21 December 2019 *Mark Timothy* waits at Coltishall as *Blickling Hall* and *Wroxham Broad* arrive with a "Steam Train to Santa" from Wroxham.

Coltishall to Wroxham

The generous loading gauge for the BVR, which comes from being built on a former standard gauge formation, can be seen here to good advantage as *Wroxham Broad* passes Oval bridge on 27 April 2015. The standard gauge bridge is generous enough to take both the footpath and the narrow gauge track.

John of Gaunt arrives at Coltishall on 30 May 2016. Again, the station building can be seen on the right.

Left: On 11 August 2008 *Blickling Hall* is also seen passing Oval bridge.

Bottom left: *Spitfire* approaches Belaugh Green crossing near Wroxham with a train from Aylsham. on 7 June 2016, as the early summer flowers are in bloom. Belaugh Green crossing is the second of the Bure Valley's ungated level crossings over a minor country road.

Opposite: *John of Gaunt* crosses the road at Belaugh Green on 1 May 2010.

Below: On 2 December 2017 *Mark Timothy* crosses the road at Belaugh Green with a train for Wroxham.

KEEP
CROSSING
CLEAR

TO CONTACT
RAILWAY
phone
01263 738889

Wroxham

Wroxham is the southern terminus of the line. The village is a short walk from the station and is the centre of the Norfolk Broads holiday area. The BVR station was built for the opening of the line and is situated alongside and a short walk from the Norwich to Sheringham 'Bittern Line' of Abellio Greater Anglia. In early 2016 the BVR undertook a major improvement programme with the installation of a second platform, a centre release road and a new water tower and crew facilities, which will all help to improve operational flexibility. It is also the location of the Friends of the Bure Valley Railway's highly successful second-hand bookshop, Bufferstop Books.

On a cold day in December 2016 the same engine whistles for the road crossing at Belaugh Green.

There is a steep climb for trains leaving Wroxham as they leave the 'Bittern Line' behind and take the former branch-line formation. *Blickling Hall* makes light work of the climb in May 2017.

Above: The new platform and centre release road at Wroxham are seen here as the same engine arrives in more clement weather conditions on 12 July 2016.

Above right: Spitfire and *Blickling Hall* await departure from Wroxham on 19 December 2018 with a 'Steam Train to Santa'. The former standard gauge signal box can be seen in the background. This was made redundant in June 2000 when the semaphore signals were replaced on the 'Bittern Line'; it was subsequently moved back from the running lines and taken over by the Wroxham Signal Box Trust as a small museum, and is open to the public on certain days.

Right: On 30 May 2016 *Wroxham Broad* awaits departure at Wroxham.

The close proximity of the 'Bittern Line' and the BVR at Wroxham can be seen here as a Class 170 DMU forming a Sheringham to Norwich working passes *John of Gaunt*.

Above: The small station building at Wroxham contains a shop and ticket office. *2nd Air Division U.S.A.A.F.* has just arrived from Aylsham in May 2019 while *Mark Timothy* waits to take the return working.

Above right: Spitfire stands beside the new water tower and crew hut at Wroxham on 30 March 2016.

Right: During an 'Everything Goes' event on 30 May 2016, *Mark Timothy* (right) has just arrived while *John of Gaunt* (left) waits to take the train back to Aylsham.

Left: Spitfire poses on Wroxham turntable with the signal box behind on 21 August 2016.

Right: The signal box gives a great view of Wroxham station and all the activity going on. On 8 September 2019, the lines of *Wroxham Broad* are shown as it is turned ready to return to Aylsham.

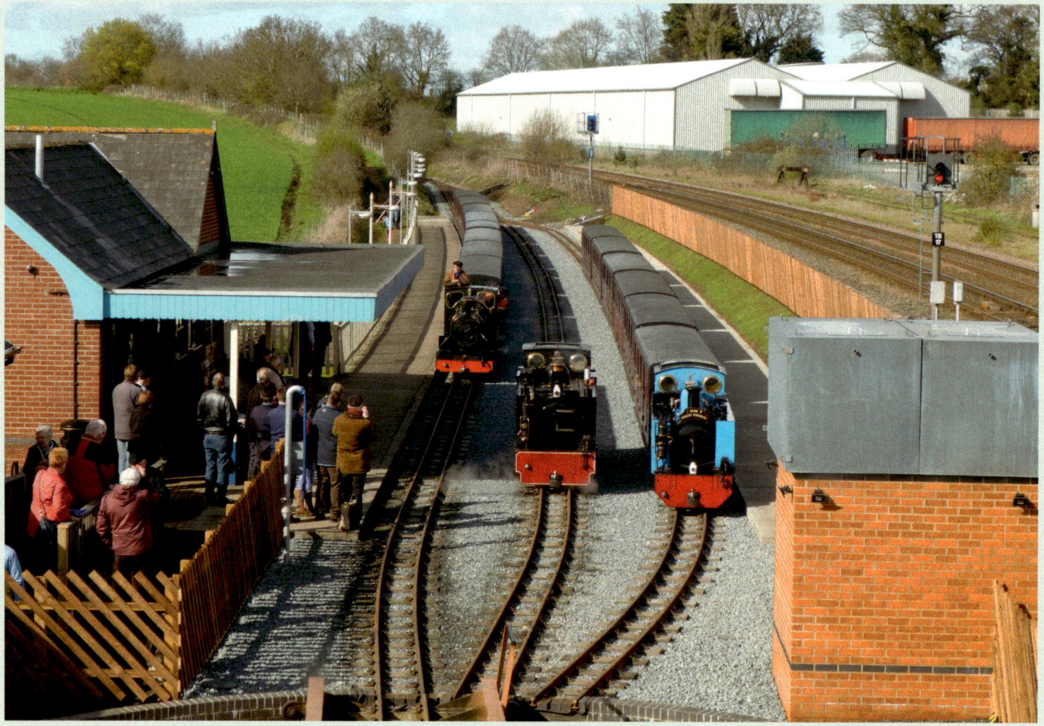

On 16 April 2016 the new layout at Wroxham was officially opened on the occasion of the AGM of the Friends of the Bure Valley Railway (the BVR's supporters association). From right to left, *Wroxham Broad* stands in the new platform having brought in the Friends' special, *John of Gaunt* stands in the middle road on test, having just returned from overhaul, while *Spitfire* pulls into Platform 1 with a service train from Aylsham.

Index